GLOBETROTTERS
NEW ZEALAND
Jane Hinchey
REDBACK publishing
I0820429

Redback Publishing
Suite 6, 13a Narabang Way,
Belrose NSW 2085
Australia

www.redbackpublishing.com
orders@redbackpublishing.com



ISBN 978-1-761401-41-1 PBK



Author: Jane Hinchey
Editor: Marlene Vaughan
Design: Redback Publishing

Original illustrations © Redback Publishing 2025
Originated by Redback Publishing

A catalogue record for this book is available from the National Library of Australia

Acknowledgements
Abbreviations: l—left, r—right, b—bottom, t—top, c—centre, m—middle
We would like to thank the following for permission to reproduce photographs: (Images © shutterstock) p7tl Yevgen Belich, p8tr Māori - Dixson Library, State Library of New South Wales, p8ml Yevgen Belich, p8br Yevgen Belich, p9br Leonard Zhukovsky, p10tr Sam Elone / http://mytongavisit.blogspot.com, p10tr Uwe Aranas, p10bl By VineStar, p12tr Tamati Waka Nene by Gottfried Lindauer via Wikimedia.com, p12ml Ricardo Barata, p13mr ChameleonsEye, p14tm riekephotos, p14m Natata, p14bl MM_photos, p16mr Hangi - Sarah Stewart / Flickr, p17tr Paolo Bona, p19br Mt Ngauruhoe by Gavin Mills from Freeimages.com, p23tl Shaun Jeffers, 24ml Featureflash Photo Agency, p24bl Nok Lek, p24br travelview, p26br mastapiece, p28ml Petr Sommer Photography, p29ml D. Pimborough, p31tr ChameleonsEye, p31ml Text and Tulip, p31br ChameleonsEye

Every effort has been made to contact copyright holders of any material reproduced in this book. Any omissions will be rectified in subsequent printings if notice is given to the publisher.

# CONTENTS

# MAP OF NEW ZEALAND

## FIVE MAJOR SITES ON THE NORTH ISLAND

Bay of Islands
FAR NORTH DISTRICT

White Island
BAY OF PLENTY

Rotorua
NORTH ISLAND

Tongariro National Park
NORTH ISLAND

AUCKLAND

NEW ZEALAND

### Can You Say This?

The longest place name in the world is New Zealand's Taumata whakatangi hangakoauau o tamatea turi pukakapiki maunga horo nuku pokai whenua kitanatahu.

# FIVE MAJOR SITES ON THE SOUTH ISLAND

Abel Tasman National Park
SOUTH ISLAND

Fox and Franz Josef Glaciers
WESTLAND, SOUTH ISLAND

Aoraki Mount Cook National Park
SOUTH ISLAND

Fiordland National Park
MILFORD SOUND

New Zealand

Lake Wakatipu
QUEENSTOWN

# WELCOME TO NEW ZEALAND

New Zealand is a small country famed for its diverse natural beauty. It is made up of two main islands, the North Island and the South Island. It is one of the least crowded countries in the world. Three-quarters of the population live on the North Island, with most people in cities like Auckland and the capital city, Wellington.

## Fun Fact

The capital city, Wellington, is the southernmost capital in the world.

The Māori are the indigenous Polynesian people of New Zealand

## Fun Fact

The Māori named New Zealand Aotearoa which means 'The Land of the Long White Cloud'.

Modern New Zealand is a multicultural society, with people from many different backgrounds. Around 300,000 New Zealanders identify as Māori, with over double that claiming some Māori heritage.

## SNAPSHOT

**COUNTRY**
New Zealand (English), Aotearoa (Māori)

**CAPITAL**
Wellington

| AREA | POPULATION |
|---|---|
| 268,021 square kilometres | 4,951,270 (March 2021) |

**OFFICIAL LANGUAGES**
English; Māori; New Zealand Sign Language

| HIGHEST POINT | Mount Cook, 3,724 metres |
|---|---|

## Did You Know?

The kiwi is a flightless bird, native to New Zealand. It is the national symbol. New Zealanders are also known as Kiwis.

# MĀORI HERITAGE

The Māori were the first inhabitants of New Zealand and arrived from Polynesia about 1,200 years ago. Māori culture is rich with songs, art, dance and deep spiritual beliefs. Today some Māori continue to live in traditional tribal areas, however most Māori live in large towns and cities.

## Māori Tattoos

Māori tattoos, or Moko, represent a person's achievements and status and are considered sacred. No two tattoos are alike.

## Māori Words

- Haere mai – welcome
- Kia ora – hello/thank you
- Tena koe – hello (to one person)
- Tena koutou – hello (to three or more people)
- Ka pai – good/excellent
- Haere ra – good bye (said by person staying)
- E noho ra – goodbye (said by person leaving)

## Traditional Dress

Traditional Māori clothes were made from animal skins and from woven flax. Ceremonial cloaks indicated status, with Chieftains wearing the finest ones. Women also wore capes and skirts made from flax. Māori wore jewellery and decorative head combs made from bone and stone.

## Did You Know?

New Zealand Sign Language (NZSL) became one of New Zealand's three official languages in 2006. It is unique because it incorporates signs for Māori concepts. It is used by more than 24,000 people in New Zealand daily.

## Traditional Crafts

Māori women weave flax mats, baskets and coverings for decoration, as well as for the tourist trade. Legend says that traditional weaving was given to Māori women by a spirit named Niwareka. Māori carvers continue the tradition of carving logs into doors and pillars.

The tiki is a human figure carved from greenstone and worn around the neck.

## Marae

The marae (meeting place) is a religious and community space where Māori people meet. It is a place where Māori community, spirituality and customs are celebrated.

# AT SCHOOL

In New Zealand, education is free and compulsory between a student's sixth and sixteenth birthday. The school year begins in late January and ends in mid-December. There are four terms each year.

## Technology in Schools

The government funds numerous programs in schools. Digital technology is taught to all students from Year 1. The six themes to be included are:

- Algorithms
- Programming
- Data representation
- Digital devices and infrastructure
- Digital applications
- Humans and computers

## Kids Voting Program

New Zealand schools can register for their students to vote in elections. While the votes aren't actually counted, it raises awareness among young people about New Zealand's election issues and the electoral processes.

# AT HOME

New Zealand is a safe, peaceful country. Three quarters of people live in single-family households. Most families have easy access to excellent schooling, healthcare and affordable housing. Young people play sports and enjoy the outdoors.

## Three Things About Kiwi Kids

The Growing Up in New Zealand longitudinal study followed 7,000 Kiwi kids for ten years.

More children now understand and speak te reo Māori.

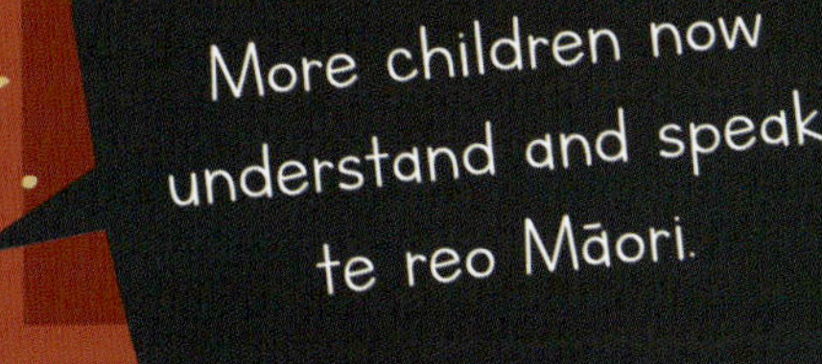

By the age of two, children in New Zealand are on digital devices for an average of two hours a day.

One in four children live in a household with extended family members in their first year of life.

# RELIGION

New Zealand has no official religion. Christians comprise the largest religious group in New Zealand, but there are also many other religious groups, including Muslim, Hindu, Sikh and Buddhist communities.

Tūmatauenga is the primary god of war and human activities such as hunting, food cultivation, fishing, and cooking

## Māori Religion

The Māori brought Polynesian religious practices with them to New Zealand. They believe in gods who represent the forces of nature, the earth and the sky. Ancestor worship is important and the Māori people believe that the spirits of their ancestors can be called on to help them in times of need.

### What's That Word?

Ancestor: a person who you are related to but who lived a long time before you were born.

# GOVERNMENT

New Zealand is a democratic country. Members of Parliament are elected by the people of New Zealand who are enrolled to vote. A central government makes decisions for the whole nation and local governments look after specific regions and districts.

## Central Government

New Zealand's central government deals with housing, welfare, education, health, energy, justice, immigration, the police and defence, foreign policy and the national road and rail systems.

## Local Government

Local government bodies oversee local services such as water, parks, rubbish collection and disposal, sewage treatment, local roads, local public transport and libraries.

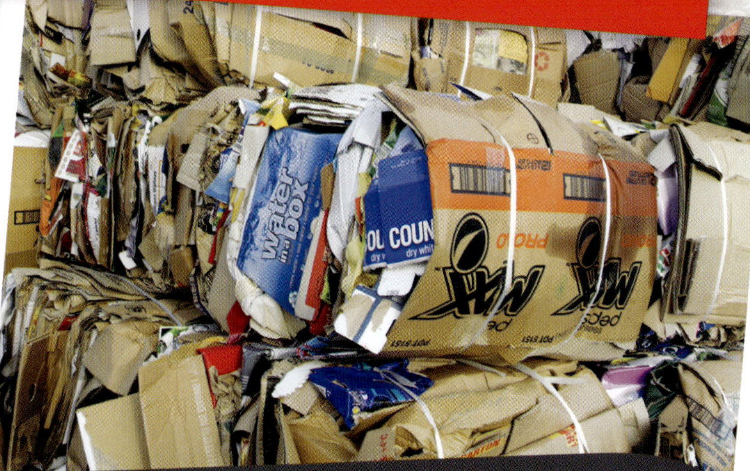

## Why Does New Zealand Have a Queen?

New Zealand's government is based on the British Westminster system and is a constitutional monarchy. The Queen of England is Head of State and represented in New Zealand by the Governor General.

# HISTORY

## The Treaty of Waitangi

The signing of the Treaty of Waitangi was an important event in New Zealand's history. It established British law in New Zealand and recognised the Māori as the traditional owners. The treaty was signed on February 6th, 1840 by Captain William Hobson, a number of English residents and 39 Māori rangatira (chieftains).

**1000-1400 AD**

The Māori arrive by canoe from the Polynesian islands.

**1642**

Abel Tasman is the first European explorer to sight New Zealand.

**1769**

James Cook makes his first voyage to the islands.

**1815**

The first British missionaries arrive.

**1840**

The Treaty of Waitangi is signed.

# First Peoples

The Māori were the first inhabitants of New Zealand, arriving by canoe from Polynesia about 1,000 years ago. They called their new home Aotearoa, which means 'Land of the Long White Cloud'. The Māori brought dogs with them and plants for food. They hunted and fished. Most settled and grew crops on the northern island, where it is warmer.

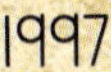

**1845–1872**
The Land Wars between Māoris and European settlers.

**1893**
New Zealand is the first country in the world to give women the right to vote.

**1947**
New Zealand gains independence from Britain.

**1997**
Jennifer Shipley becomes the country's first female Prime Minister.

**2011**
A major earthquake causes widespread damage in Christchurch.

**2017**
Jacinda Ardern becomes the 40th Prime Minister of New Zealand.

# FOOD

New Zealand has rich soil, and clean air and water. The climate is perfect for dairy cattle and the dairy industry produces excellent cheeses and butter.

New Zealand produces a variety of meats, and lamb is especially popular. Being an island nation, seafood such as marlin, mussels, trout, crayfish and blue cod play an important role, as do shellfish. Some oysters are specific to certain areas.

## Hāngi

Hāngi is a traditional Māori meal that is cooked in an earth oven. Hot rocks are placed in a pit with meat and vegetables on top, which are then covered with earth so the heat does not escape. After about six hours, the earth is removed and the food is ready.

Traditional Māori foods that are often cooked in a hāngi include pipi, tuatua, freshwater eel and other fish, fern fronds and roots, sweet potatoes and wild birds.

### Kiwis For Kiwis

Kiwi fruit is the main product of the organics industry.

# A SPORTING NATION

Kiwis love their sport and participate in a wide range including netball, cricket, soccer and golf. Rugby union is considered New Zealand's national sport.

## The Beloved All Blacks

New Zealand's national rugby union team is known as the All Blacks. They are consistent high performers, often rising to be the number one team in the world. The All Blacks are famous for performing the haka before each match.

New Zealand has some of the most spectacular ski fields in the world and skiing and snowboarding are popular winter sports. The Winter Games take place every two years in New Zealand's Southern Alps.

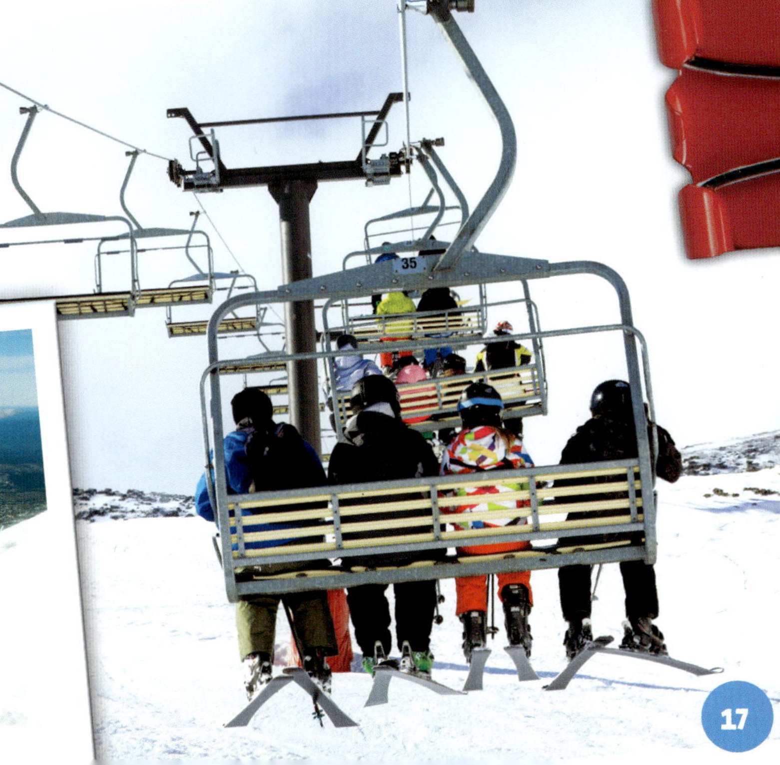

# WEATHER AND LANDSCAPE

## Climate

New Zealand's temperature is subtropical in the far north but temperate and cool further south. The warmest months are January and February and the coldest are July and August. New Zealand's average rainfall is high (600 - 1,600 millimetres) and evenly spread throughout the year.

New Zealand is made up of two major landmasses and a number of smaller islands. The North Island and South Island are separated by the Cook Strait.

## Glaciers

New Zealand contains many slow moving rivers of ice, called glaciers. There are over 3,000 smaller glaciers on the North Island, but the truly stunning ones are on the South Island, around the Southern Alps. Tasman Glacier near Mount Cook is 27 kilometres long.

## South Island

The South Island is divided by the Southern Alps that loom over the fjords and glaciers. The South Island is larger than the North Island, but less populated.

## North Island

The North Island is less mountainous than the South Island. In the central region lies the North Island Volcanic Plateau and the steaming geysers and volcanoes of the Rotorua region.

## Earthquakes

New Zealand is situated in the Pacific 'Ring of Fire'. Every year about 15,000 earthquakes are recorded in New Zealand, but only 100 to 150 are large enough to be felt. In 2011, a 6.3 magnitude earthquake hit Christchurch.

## Fun Fact

New Zealand is the first country in the world to see the sun each day.

## Did You Know?

The tectonic plates under New Zealand push together, causing the Southern Alps to grow up to eight millimetres a year.

## Volcanoes

New Zealand has a number of active volcanoes in what is known as the Taupo Volcanic Zone, on the North Island and some offshore islands. The last huge eruption took place at Taupo about 1,800 years ago.

# WILDLIFE

New Zealand has many unique animals, found nowhere else in the world.

## Flightless Birds

It is thought that some birds did not develop wings because they had no natural predators to escape from. Many animals have since been introduced that threaten these flightless birds. The most famous native bird is the kiwi, after which New Zealanders are now named.

### Famous Kiwi Fun Fact

The female kiwi lays her eggs, and her mate incubates them for 11 weeks - the longest known incubation period of any bird.

Critically endangered: kakapo

Already extinct: moa

The yellow-eyed penguin is only found in New Zealand and nowhere else in the world!

## Marine Life

New Zealand's countless bays, inlets, harbours and estuaries are home to hundreds of marine species, many unique to the region. Marine mammals include whales, seals and dolphins. Hector's dolphin is one of the smallest dolphins in the world.

### Fact Box

There are no poisonous snakes or spiders in New Zealand, apart from the Katipō (an endangered spider).

# INDUSTRY

New Zealand's small size and geographical location poses challenges for it competing on the global export market. Australia is its biggest trading partner.

## Imports

New Zealand's top three imports are machinery, vehicles and oil.

Its major import partners are China, Australia and the US.

## Exports

New Zealand's top three exports are dairy, meat and wood.

New Zealand is the world's largest exporter of dairy products and lamb.

# TOURISM

Shotover River
QUEENSTOWN

New Zealand is a popular tourist destination. Travellers flock to places like Queenstown, Milford Sound, Rotorua and Auckland. Whether you're after a relaxing holiday or an adrenaline-packed adventure, New Zealand has it all.

## Did You Know?

The Māori never climbed Mt Cook (Aoraki), because they believed it to be sacred.

## Thrill Seekers

New Zealand is famous for its adventure activities such as white-water rafting, skiing, snowboarding and bungee jumping. A New Zealander named A J Hackett introduced bungee jumping to the world. In 1998, he set a world record when bungee jumping off Auckland's Sky Tower.

Sky Tower
AUCKLAND

# NOTABLE PEOPLE

## Peter Jackson

Peter Jackson is a multi-award-winning film director. He began his career making 'splatstick' horror films, but is best known for his big budget features like King Kong and The Lord of the Rings trilogy, which won eleven Oscars.

Jackson's Wellington-based film and digital effects company, Weta Digital, has been behind dozens of major Hollywood films, bringing work to New Zealand. In 2012, he was made Knight Companion (KNZM) and received the order of New Zealand (ONZ).

The Lord of the Rings movie set is a popular tourist destination

MATAMATA, NEW ZEALAND

Peter Jackson's star on the Hollywood Walk of Fame

LOS ANGELES, USA

## Dame Kiri Te Kanawa

Born March 6, 1944 in Gisborne, Kiri Te Kanawa is a Māori opera singer. She has had a successful international career with performances at London's Covent Garden and New York's Metropolitan Opera.

In 1981, Kiri Te Kanawa sang at the wedding of Prince Charles and Lady Diana Spencer, to a televised audience of 600 million.

She became a Dame Commander of the Order of the British Empire (DBE) in 1982.

Dame Kiri Te Kanawa
ARTS FOUNDATION ICON AWARDS 2013

## Hone Tuwhare (1922-2008)

Hone Tuwhare is New Zealand's most respected Māori poet. His first collection, *No Ordinary Sun*, was published in 1964 to wide acclaim. Twelve more collections followed over the following forty years.

In 1999, Hone Tuwhare was named New Zealand Te Mata Poet Laureate and in 2003 was named one of New Zealand's ten greatest living artists. *No Ordinary Sun* is still taught in New Zealand schools today.

# Sir Edmund Hillary

(1919 - 2008)

Sir Edmund Hillary was an explorer and mountaineer. In 1953, along with Sherpa Tenzing Norgay, he was the first person to reach the summit of Mount Everest. In 1960, he founded the Himalayan Trust, which had a focus on supporting the Sherpas of Nepal by building health clinics and schools. He received many awards and accolades, including Knight of the Order of the Garter (KG), Companion of the Order of New Zealand (ONZ), and Knight Commander of the Order of the British Empire (KBE).

**Mount Everest and climbers**
NEPALESE HIMALAYAS

# Sir Āpirana Turupa Ngata

(1874 - 1950)

Born to a Scottish mother and a Māori father who was a tribal leader and expert in traditional lore, Ngata became a prominent Māori lawyer and politician. He was the first Māori to graduate from university and used his degree to create social and economic changes and promote land reforms for his people. He was also a Liberal Member of Parliament for many years.

Ngata promoted Māori arts and was instrumental in the establishment of the Māori Arts and Crafts Institute at Rotorua in 1927, and the construction of decorated meeting-houses around the country. In recognition of his services to the Māori people, Ngata was knighted in 1927.

The New Zealand Māori Arts and Crafts Institute

ROTORUA, NEW ZEALAND

# TRANSPORT

## Plane

New Zealand is an island nation, so travel by air is a popular choice. Air New Zealand is the national carrier, with an extensive international network. New Zealand has seven international airports: Auckland, Hamilton, Dunedin, Christchurch, Wellington, Palmerston North and Queenstown.

Flights between major domestic airports are often the easiest way to traverse New Zealand's rugged terrain. Domestic carriers include Air New Zealand, Jetstar and a number of regional airlines.

## Car

The most convenient way to travel around New Zealand is by road. The country has a good road system and highways link the main cities, with amazing scenery along the way. Off the main highways, roads can be narrow and drivers need to be alert to any extreme weather in the area.

## Train

Travelling by train is a great way to see the country. Both Auckland and Wellington have commuter trains, and there are also long distance train services.

The Wellington cable car is widely recognised as a symbol of Wellington

## Ship

Ships move freight in and out of New Zealand from international seaports. Commercial fishing is an important industry, as is the provision of transport by boats and ferries. Large ferries take passengers between the North and South Islands, on a trip that takes over three hours.

PICTON, NEW ZEALAND

# FLAGS AND SPECIAL DAYS

## Flag of New Zealand

The New Zealand flag has a royal blue background derived from the ensign of the Blue Squadron of the Royal Navy. The stars of the Southern Cross signify New Zealand's location in the South Pacific Ocean.

In 2010 on Waitangi Day, the national Māori flag was officially recognised by 47 countries.

The Beehive, also known as the Executive Wing, is one of four parliament buildings

WELLINGTON, NEW ZEALAND

# Special Days

New Zealand celebrates numerous public holidays throughout the year, including local and regional ones. Some of the more important national holidays include:

## Waitangi Day

(February 6)

Commemorates the signing of the Treaty of Waitangi.

## ANZAC Day

(April 25)

A public holiday in New Zealand and Australia, commemorating those who have served and died in all wars, conflicts and peacekeeping operations.

## National Anthem

Officially, both *God Defend New Zealand* and *God Save the Queen* are New Zealand's national anthems. *God Defend New Zealand* is sung on public occasions with both English and Māori lyrics.

# GLOSSARY

**ancestors** people who are related to you but lived a long time before you were born

**endangered** when a species is at risk

**glacier** mass or river of ice that is constantly moving forward

**hangi** traditional Māori meal cooked in an earth oven

**independence** when a country is ruled by its own people

**māori** original inhabitants of New Zealand

**tectonic plates** large pieces of the Earth's cust that move across the globe

**Pacific Ring of Fire** area in and around the Pacific Ocean where earthquakes and volcanoes are common

**Sherpa** Tibetan or Nepalese guide skilled at mountaineering, known for assisting climbers on Mount Everest

# INDEX